Fifty Shades of Bacon

Benjamin Myhre

Jenna Johnson

Table of Contents

Foreplay
"Appetizers"

Afternoon Delight
"Main Course"

Multiple Orgasms
"Dessert"

Bacon Fudge   30
Bacon Lattice Apple Pie   31
Bacon S'mores   32
Chocolate Covered Bacon   33
Chocolate Covered Bacon Ice Cream   34

The Morning Wood
"Breakfast"

Bacon Cheddar Scones   37
Bacon Cheddar Waffle Sandwiches   38
Bacon & Egg Breakfast Tacos   39
Bacon Egg & Biscuit Cups   40
Bacon Jam   41
Bacon Pancake Donuts   42
Bacon Quiche   43
Fig & Bacon Pop Tarts   44

Bondage
"Miscellaneous"

Bacon Bits   47
Bacon Brown Sugar Rub   48
Bacon Butter   49
Bacon Cupcake Martini   50
Bacon Extract   51
Bacon Mayonnaise   52
Bacon Peanut Butter   53
Bacon Pesto   54
Bacon Popcorn   55
Bacon Ranch Dip   56
Brown Sugar Bacon   57
Creamy Garlic Bacon Dip   58

I had just signed the contract today and now I am naked; kneeling in the corner of Hamastasia Pink's red kitchen. She had ordered me to look at the floor, so all I am doing is sitting here waiting and looking down. I am scared, excited and thrilled all at the same time. Most of all, however, I am hungry.

My youth was spent in a strict vegan colony and Hamastasia is the first to show me the pleasures of pork. Now, I, Benjamin Bradly Queue, am a slave to my mistress and her kitchen...here to learn about the Fifty Shades of Bacon. With my eyes down, I hear her walking toward me. Finally, I see her girthy ankles and slightly swollen feet place themselves right in front of me.

"Are you ready to begin, Mr. BBQ?" she asks.

"Yes." Suddenly, I see a swift hand arch down with a plastic spatula and strike me on the leg. Hamastasia's time as an Olympic shotputter was very evident and her strong hand shows who runs this kitchen. "Yes, what?" she asks.

"Yes, ma'am."

"Good.... good. You are learning."

My eyes are still pointing down and then my mistress drops it. A large package of Bacon falls between my legs. She extends a scissors and tells me to open the package. I follow her directions. After I have the package open, Hamastasia says, "Stand up Mr. BBQ and make your way to the stove top. Lay the Bacon on the griddle and turn it up to medium high. Remain standing there." I follow her directions.

She continues speaking to me and telling me about the recipes we will make, but I am too busy thinking about the meal that will follow. My half erection soon begins to fall as I realize that the Bacon is beginning to sizzle. Very small droplets of Bacon grease is beginning to pop up and land on my bare chest and even my penis.

This isn't fun anymore, but I desire the treasure of her Bacon secrets.

"Do you still like me, Mr. BBQ?" Hamastasia asks.

"Ahhh... Ow... Umm this hurts, ma'am", I replied. Her Olympian muscles swung the plastic spatula on my bare buttocks.

"Answer my question!"

"Yes, ma'am!"

"Mr. BBQ, you have signed a contract and now you are in my service. Here is your guide book." She placed a cookbook beside the stovetop so that I could see. Fifty Shades of Bacon. "We will explore the erotic nature of Bacon and I will teach you everything I know. I will release you from my service when you have completed all 50 recipes."

This begins my service and learning the Fifty Shades of Bacon.

Foreplay
"Appetizers"

Bacon Deviled Eggs

10 hard boiled eggs

¼ C mayonnaise

1 Tbsp dijon mustard

1 Tbsp fresh chives; chopped

5 slices Bacon, chopped

Boil eggs. *(see below for instruction)*

Cut the hard boiled eggs in half. Scoop out the yoke and place inside a food processor. Add the mayonnaise, dijon mustard, and chopped chives and pulse a couple times in the food processor until well combined.

Fill the eggs with the mixture and sprinkle with cooked Bacon.

How to boil eggs:

Place eggs in single layer in saucepan. Cover with at least one inch of cold water over tops of shells. Cover pot with lid and bring to a boil over medium heat.

As soon as the water comes to a full boil, remove from heat and let stand. Let stand in hot water 15 to 17 minutes.

Drain off hot water. Immediately cover with cold water and add a few ice cubes. Let stand in cold water until completely cooled.

Bacon Pasta Salad

1 lb of Bacon

1 16 oz package of spiral pasta

1 C mayonnaise

½ C white sugar

¼ C white vinegar

1 medium onion, chopped

¾ C celery, chopped

½ C carrots, shredded

½ tsp pepper

1 tsp salt

Cook Bacon as directed for Bacon bits *(see page 47).*

Cook pasta as directed on package and allow to cool.

In a large bowl, add all ingredients (set some of the Bacon bits aside for garnish) and mix until fully blended.

Cover and store in the refrigerator for at least 4 hours before serving.

Before serving, sprinkle remaining Bacon on top as garnish.

Bacon Wrapped Asparagus with Creamy Gorgonzola Sauce

10 asparagus

10 slices of peppered Bacon

3 Tbsp butter

1 clove garlic, minced

½ C cream

¾ C crumbled gorgonzola cheese

1 Tbsp green onions, chopped

Wash and cut bottoms off of asparagus.

Wrap the Bacon around the asparagus. Only the asparagus tips should be showing.

Place on a baking sheet. Preheat oven to 400 degrees. When the oven is close to preheat temperature, add butter and garlic to medium sauce pan at medium heat.

Place the Bacon wrapped asparagus in oven and bake for approximately 17 minutes or until Bacon is done.

While Bacon is cooking and once butter has melted, add cream to pan and continually stir. Slowly add cheese to cream and stir in until melted.

Once Bacon is done, add asparagus to plate and drizzle with cheese sauce. Sprinkle with green onions and serve.

Bacon Wrapped Pickles

10 kosher dill pickles

10 slices uncooked Bacon

Preheat your deep fryer to 350 degrees.

Wrap the bacon around the pickles.

Drop the pickles into the deep fryer until the Bacon is cooked or crispy, or until the pickles float to the top.

Blue Cheese Stuffed Figs Wrapped in Proscuitto

1 pint fresh figs

1 container crumbled blue cheese

6 oz thinly sliced prosciutto

Cut figs in half.

Place some blue cheese in the center of the fig and wrap with the prosciutto.

Grill the figs on each side for 3 minutes or until the cheese is melted in the middle and the Bacon prosciutto is crispy.

Healthy Potato Skins

4 medium sized russet potatoes

4 oz of light cheddar cheese

8 Tbsp fat free sour cream

4 slices Bacon, chopped

2 green onions, chopped

cooking spray

salt & pepper

Preheat oven to 400 degrees. Spray potatoes with cooking spray and season with salt and pepper. Bake for 30 to 40 minutes.

Take the potatoes out of the oven. Cut them in half. Scoop out the insides so there's just enough potato around the skin. Use potato insides for something else.

Spray the potatoes again with cooking spray to give them more flavor. Lay them on their flat side on the baking sheet and bake again for an additional 10 minutes.

Take them out of oven and sprinkle with cheese. Place back in the oven until the cheese is melted.

Top with ingredients such as sour cream, Bacon and green onions.

Meat Candy

1 package little smokies

1 lb Bacon

1 C brown sugar

Preheat oven to 375.

Cut Bacon slices in half and wrap around little smokies.

Secure little smokies with a toothpick.

Season the little smokies with brown sugar.

Cook in 9 x 13 baking dish for 15 to 20 minutes.

Spicy Bacon Wrapped Shrimp

20 jumbo shrimp

10 strips Bacon

½ C sriracha sauce

¼ C honey

⅛ C brown sugar

salt & pepper

toothpicks

Season shrimp with salt and pepper.

Cut strips of Bacon in half.

Wrap the Bacon around peeled and deveined shrimp and insert a toothpick in the middle of the shrimp and Bacon so the Bacon stays on the shrimp.

Combine sriracha sauce, honey, and brown sugar. Marinade shrimp in the sriracha and honey sauce for 20 minutes.

Cook the shrimp wrapped with Bacon on a non-stick skillet. About 5 minutes on each side, until Bacon is fully cooked.

Stuffed Wontons with Cream Cheese & Bacon

20 wonton wrappers (small size)

1 8 oz container of Philadelphia
   cream cheese

1 tsp fresh chives, chopped

5 strips cooked Bacon, chopped

olive oil

In a small bowl combine the cream cheese, chives and Bacon.

Place about 1 to 2 teaspoons of the cream cheese mixture in the middle of the wonton.

Dampen the edges of the wonton wrapper with water and fold the wonton into a triangle.

Place the wontons stuffed with cream cheese on a cookie sheet, spray or brush with olive oil and bake in the oven.

Bake at 400 degrees for 10 minutes or until the crust of the wonton wrapper is golden brown.

Afternoon Delight

"Main Course"

Awesome Bacon Meatloaf

1 lb hamburger

1 lb spicy Italian pork sausage

1 lb Bacon

1 C ketchup

2 Tbsp brown sugar

2 eggs

1 C bread crumbs

salt & pepper

Preheat oven to 350.

Mix ketchup and brown sugar together in a small bowl and set aside.

Take half of the Bacon and chop, but keep the other half as whole strips.

In large bowl, combine ½ of the ketchup/sugar mixture. Add all of the the hamburger, pork sausage, chopped Bacon, eggs and bread crumbs. Mix these all together very well. Add salt and pepper as desired.

On baking sheet or large loaf pan, lay out mixture in loaf form. Take remaining Bacon strips and wrap the loaf with the Bacon. Then, coat the loaf with the remaining ketchup/brown sugar mixture.

Place in oven and cook for 1 hour or until internal temperature reaches 170.

Remove from oven and allow to stand for 5 minutes.

Bacon Alfredo

1 package pasta, any kind

8 oz Bacon

¼ C butter

1 clove garlic, chopped

1½ C heavy cream

1½ C parmesan cheese

¼ C gorgonzola cheese (optional)

pepper to taste

Place Bacon in freezer just long enough to become firm and easier to chop. Once half frozen, cut the Bacon into ¼ inch pieces.

In large pan, fry the Bacon over medium high heat until done and allow to dry on a paper towel.

Cook pasta as directed on package.

While Bacon is draining, add butter and garlic to pan at medium low heat. Once butter melts, add cream slowly and continually stir. Turn heat up a little and slowly add cheeses into pan and continuously stir. Add 6 ounces of Bacon and stir into sauce that should be thickening.

Stir into hot pasta, dish and garnish with remaining Bacon.

Bacon Feta Pizza

Dough:

2 C bread flour

¼ oz yeast mix

1 C warm water

1 tsp sugar

1 tsp salt

2 Tbsp extra virgin olive oil

Sauce:

16 oz stewed tomatoes

½ medium onion

2 cloves garlic

1 tsp oregano

1/2 tsp salt

Toppings:

1 C pizza mix cheese

1 C feta cheese

1 C Bacon bits *(see page 47)*

Other equipment:

1 pizza stone

1 pizza peel

Prepare dough 24 hours in advance. Add yeast to one cup of warm water and allow to sit for ten minutes.

In a large bowl add flour, sugar, EVOO and salt. Add in water and yeast and mix until well incorporated. Add additional water or flour and mix until the consistency of uncooked pizza dough. It should be somewhat firm and not flaky. Knead into a small smooth disc. Sprinkle outside with flour. Cover and place dough in a dark place to rise for one hour. After the hour, re-knead dough and once again make it into a disc. Cover in bowl and store in refrigerator for approximately 24 hours (up to 2 days).

Sauce – Blend all sauce ingredients together. Add to sauce pan and simmer until the sauce reduces to a thicker consistency. This can be done the day of making pizza, but can also be made the same day as the dough and stored in the refrigerator.

Add pizza stone to oven and preheat oven to 550F. Allow to heat for at least 15 minutes after reaching temperature.

Roll out dough and fit onto your pizza peel. Generously add flour to peel to help prevent sticking. Add sauce leaving room around the edges for crust. Also, at this point, make sure your pizza still slides. Add both cheeses evenly around the pizza and then apply Bacon. Slide the pizza onto the stone (in the oven) and cook 6-10 minutes or until cheese and crust turns a golden baked brown.

BLT with Mayo Spread

1 bagel

2 Tbsp Philadelphia chive
   cream cheese

2 strips Bacon

1 lettuce leaf

2 slices tomato

Toast the bagel.

Spread with Philadelphia cream cheese or the Bacon mayonaisse *(see page 52).*

Top with 2 slices of Bacon, tomato, and lettuce.

Bacon Taco Pizza

1 store bought pizza dough

1 8 oz package cream cheese

1 package taco seasoning

½ C cheddar cheese

½ head lettuce, shredded

1 whole tomato, diced

6 strips Bacon, chopped

Bake the pizza crust according to package directions; Pillsbury Artisian is delicious.

In a bowl combine the cream cheese and taco seasoning and spread that over the cooled pizza crust.

Top with remaining taco ingredients. Add whatever other taco toppings you like on your pizza.

Bacon Wrapped Maple Chicken

4 chicken breasts

½ C maple syrup

¼ C dijon mustard

2 Tbsp soy sauce

1 Tbsp garlic, minced

1 tsp sriracha sauce

8 slices Bacon

salt & pepper

Season chicken with salt and pepper.

Wrap chicken with 2 slices of Bacon depending on how large the chicken breast is.

In a bowl combine the maple syrup, mustard, soy sauce, garlic and sriracha sauce together. Pour the mixture over the chicken breasts in a 9 x 13 baking dish. Bake at 400 degrees for 20 to 25 minutes or until chicken is cooked through.

Bacon Wrapped Fish

4 large fish fillets such as pollock

8 slices of Bacon

salt & pepper

Season fish with salt and pepper. Wrap 2 slices of Bacon around each fillet.

Cook the fish in a skillet or in the oven until the Bacon and fish is cooked through. About 5 minutes per side in the skillet.

To add a bit more Bacon flavor serve with Bacon Mayonnaise *(see page 52)*.

Bacon Wrapped Stuffed Cheeseburger

1½ lb ground beef

2 Tbsp grill seasoning

    such as Weber

1 lb Bacon

8 oz cheddar cheese

4 hamburger buns

1 head lettuce

2 tomatoes, sliced

toothpicks

Preheat a grill.

Season burger with seasoning and divide the ground beef into 4 equal burger patties.

In the center of the patty, add some cheddar cheese and fold the patty in half.

Re-shape the burger again. Wrap the burger with Bacon until it's completely covered in it.

Secure the burger and Bacon with a toothpick.

Cook the burgers on the grill until however well done you like them. Top with lettuce and tomato and place on a burger bun.

Bacon Mac N' Cheese

½ lb elbow macaroni

½ lb Bacon bits *(see page 47)*

1 C + 1 Tbsp butter

3 Tbsp flour

2 C cream

1 C shredded cheddar cheese

1 C monterey jack cheese, shredded

1 tsp salt

Fresh, cracked pepper to taste

¾ C bread crumbs

Cook pasta as directed on package and set aside.

Preheat oven to 375.

In separate pot set to medium high, melt ¾ cup of butter. Add salt, pepper and flour. Slowly stir in cream and continually stir and reduce temperature to keep mixture just below boiling point. Slowly add cheeses, while continually stiring. Once the cheese is completely blended, add Bacon to the sauce.

Combine sauce and pasta together and thoroughly mix. Butter a baking dish with 1 tablespoon of butter and add mixture to dish.

In separate pot, melt remaining butter and toss in bread crumbs. Top the macaroni with bread crumbs and cook in oven for 25 minutes.

Beefy Bacon Chili

1 lb hamburger

½ lb Bacon

1 quart stewed tomatoes

1 Tbsp extra virgin olive oil

1 onion, chopped

3 cloves garlic, minced

1 jalapeño, diced

1 can chilli beans

3 oz chilli powder

½ C milk

Fry Bacon per instructions on package and brown burger and set aside.

In large pan, add olive oil and heat to medium. Add onions, garlic and jalepeno and cook until onions are translucent. Once translucent, add to blender with tomatoes and blend until liquified.

In large pot at medium heat, add cooked bacon and burger. Add beans and chili powder. Mix until blended and everything is warm.

Add contents from blender and simmer entire mixture for 45 minutes. Add milk and continue warming for 15 minutes.

Filet Mignon

4 filet mignon steaks

4 strips Bacon

2 Tbsp extra virgin olive oil

salt & pepper

4 toothpicks

Wrap steaks in Bacon and use toothpicks to hold in place.

Brush the steaks with the olive oil. Lightly cover both sides in salt and pepper. Allow to stand for at least 30 minutes in refrigerator before cooking.

Fire one side of the grill to be very hot and the other side to be medium low. Once heated, using tongs, sear each side of the steaks for 45 seconds on the hot side.

Once seared, place on the low side for 3 minutes and then flip. After another 3 minutes on the other side, the steak should be medium rare, but gently touch to test. Roughly, if you touch your thumb to your middle finger, that is what a medium rare steak will feel like.

Once done, remove steaks from grill and loosely cover in tinfoil. Allow to rest for 5 minutes and serve.

Potato Bacon Au Gratin

¾ C onion, chopped

1 garlic clove, minced

4 medium thinly sliced russet

    potatoes

6 strips Bacon, chopped

3 Tbsp butter

3 Tbsp flour

pepper to taste

1½ C 2% milk

2 C sharp cheddar cheese

Fry Bacon as directed until crispy and set aside to cool and drain. Also set aside one tablespoon of the Bacon grease for the sauce.

Preheat oven to 350. In lightly greased 2 Quart oven safe dish, spread garlic evenly on bottom. Add one layer of potato, then sprinkle part of onion and then 3 crumbled strips of Bacon. Repeat until these ingredients are used, but set aside a few strips of Bacon for garnish.

In a medium sauce pan, melt butter on low heat. Stir in flour and pepper until smooth. Add milk and continue to heat and stir until warm. Add the cheese and Bacon grease to milk. Stir until smooth.

Pour sauce mixture over potatoes. Cover with tinfoil and place in oven for 1 hour and 15 minutes. If potatoes are tender, remove tinfoil and cook 15 more minutes.

Once done, top with remaining Bacon.

Spicy Bacon Grilled Cheese Sandwich

2 slices of bread of your choice

2 slices pepper jack cheese

4 slices Bacon

1 Tbsp butter

Cook the 4 strips of Bacon as directed on package and allow to rest on paper towel to drain for 15 minutes.

Empty Bacon grease from pan, but no need to clean it entirely.

Place the Bacon and cheese in the slices of bread and use the butter to liberally coat the outside of the bread.

Heat pan to medium and place sandwich on heat Cook for 3 minutes or bottom side is golden brown. Flip and cook other side until golden brown and cheese has melted. Remove from heat once cheese is melted.

Multiple Orgasms

"Dessert"

Bacon Chocolate Chip Cookies

2¼ C flour

1 tsp baking soda

½ C + 2 Tbsp butter

2 Tbsp Bacon grease

¾ C brown sugar

¼ C sugar

1 (3.4 oz) package instant
    vanilla pudding

2 eggs

1 tsp vanilla

1 C chocolate chips

5 slices of cooked Bacon, chopped

Preheat oven to 350 F. Stir together flour and baking soda and set aside.

In a large bowl blend butter, Bacon grease and sugars together.

Add in pudding package and beat until well blended.

Add eggs and vanilla.

Add dry mixture slowly to the wet mixture until well incorporated.

Stir in chocolate chips and cooked Bacon.

Roll into 1 inch balls and place on greased baking sheet.

Bake at 350 F for 8-12 minutes.

Bacon Chocolate Cupcakes for 2

1 Tbsp butter, softened

2 Tbsp sugar

1 Tbsp egg substitute

6 Tbsp flour

1 Tbsp cocoa powder

A pinch of salt

1/16 tsp baking soda

3 Tbsp milk

Bacon Chocolate Frosting:

1 Tbsp Bacon grease

1 Tbsp butter

½ C powdered sugar

1 Tbsp cocoa powder

1 tsp milk

Bacon Bits *(see page 47)*

In a medium sized bowl, beat the butter and sugar together. Mix in the egg substitute.

In another bowl, combine flour, cocoa powder, salt and baking soda.

Gradually add in the dry ingredients to the butter and sugar mixture. Stir in milk whenever the batter is too thick.

Bake in 350 degree oven for 20 minutes.

For Frosting:

In a bowl, combine the Bacon grease, butter, powdered sugar, cocoa powder and milk.

Mix the frosting together with a hand held mixer. Frost the cupcakes and sprinkle with Bacon bits.

Bacon Chocolate Milkshake

4 C vanilla ice cream

¼ C chocolate syrup

1½ C milk

5 slices Bacon, crispy

In a blender combine all the ingredients until smooth.

Bacon Fudge

1 bag semi-sweet chocolate chips
(12 oz)

1 can sweetened condensed milk

6 strips Bacon

Cook Bacon until crispy, chop. Set aside on paper towels to drain.

Melt chocolate chips in a microwave safe bowl for 2 minutes.

Mix sweetened condensed milk and chocolate until well combined and add in the Bacon. Leave a little Bacon to top the fudge with. Pour the melted chocolate and Bacon mixture into an 8 x 8 pan and top with leftover Bacon. Let cool in the fridge until the fudge is set.

Bacon Lattice Apple Pie

1 store bought pie crust

1 jar apple pie filling

10 slices Bacon

Preheat oven to 400 degrees.

Place pie crust in the bottom of a pie pan and smooth the apple pie filling over the crust.

Place 5 strips of Bacon on top of the crust, vertically.

Weave 5 more strips of Bacon horizontally into the already laid Bacon. It should look like a basket weave.

Bake apple pie for 40 minutes. Serve with Chocolate Covered Bacon Ice Cream *(see page 34)*.

Bacon S'mores

5 strips chocolate covered Bacon

   (see page 33)

1 bag large marshmallows

1 package graham crackers

Cut the Bacon in large enough strips to fit the size of graham cracker.

Roast the marshmallows.

Make a sandwich. 1st layer graham cracker, 2nd layer chocolate covered Bacon, 3rd layer is marshmallows, and top with another graham cracker.

Chocolate Covered Bacon

1 bag chocolate chips

1 lb Bacon

Melt chocolate chips in a microwave safe bowl for 2 minutes or until the chocolate chips have melted.

Dip the cooked Bacon in the melted chocolate and place on a wire rack until cool.

Chocolate Covered Bacon Ice Cream

1½ C heavy cream

1½ C milk

1 vanilla bean

4 egg yolks

2 egg whites

1 C sugar

5 strips chocolate covered Bacon

(see page 33)

In a sauce pan combine the heavy cream, milk and vanilla bean.

While the milk is heating whisk together the eggs and sugar.

Once the milk and heavy cream have come to a boil, whisk in the eggs and sugar slowly stirring constantly so the eggs don't scramble. If any of the eggs scramble strain them out.

Let the ice cream batter cool until your ice cream maker is ready to be used.

While the ice cream is churning in the ice cream maker, stir in pieces of chopped chocolate covered Bacon.

The Morning Wood

"Breakfast"

Bacon Cheddar Scones

1½ C flour

1 tsp baking soda

1 tsp baking powder

½ tsp salt

3 Tbsp cold butter

½ C cheddar cheese

5 slices Bacon, chopped

½ C low fat butter milk

Cook Bacon as directed on package. Allow to drain on paper towel. Set aside.

Preheat oven to 450.

In a food processor combine flour, soda, baking powder, salt and butter. Pulse 3 times or until butter resembles peas. Add in cheddar, and chopped Bacon. Gradually add milk until the dough comes together to form a ball.

Roll out dough about 8 inches round. Cut 8 wedges and brush egg wash on top of the scones. This will help them get that golden color on top.

Place on greased cookie sheet and bake for 10- 12 minutes.

Bacon Cheddar Waffle Sandwiches

1 store bought container waffle mix
   or frozen waffles

8 oz cheddar cheese

10 slices Bacon

1 C maple syrup, optional

Cook Bacon fully and drain on paper towel.

Prepare your waffles as directed on package, then heat oven to 400 degrees.

Cut one waffle in half or use two whole ones. Layer some cheddar cheese and 2 slices of Bacon in the middle. Place another waffle on top of the Bacon and cheese.

Place the waffle sandwich in the oven on cookie sheet until the cheese has melted. About 5 minutes. Remove the waffle sandwich and top with as much maple syrup as you like.

Bacon & Egg Breakfast Tacos

1 package tator tots

Lawry's seasoning salt

6 large eggs

salt & pepper

1 package soft shell tacos

1 jar queso dip or nacho cheese,
    warmed in the microwave

4 slices Bacon, chopped

Cook tator tots according to package directions. Season the potatoes with Lawry's seasoning salt.

Whisk eggs in a small bowl, add salt and pepper. Cook on a stove top until the eggs are scrambled.

Assemble the taco. Place some of the scrambled eggs, nacho cheese, tator tots and Bacon on a soft shell.

Bacon Egg & Biscuit Cups

1 can buttermilk biscuits

12 slices Bacon

Eggs

1 tsp of both salt & pepper

Cooking Spray

Preheat oven to 375. Spray muffin pan with cooking spray.

In a 12 hole muffin pan, press 1 biscuit into each hole. Repeat until you have used all biscuits

Place 1 strip of Bacon, cut in half lengthwise, over the biscuit dough.

Cook the biscuits and Bacon for 10 minutes.

Take the biscuits out of the oven and crack an egg on top of each muffin. You will need the same amount of eggs as you have biscuits. Season with salt and pepper.

Place the biscuits back in the oven and bake until the egg whites have set but the yolks are runny, approximately 5 minutes.

Bacon Jam

1½ lbs sliced Bacon, cut into
    1-inch pieces

2 medium yellow onions, diced

3 garlic cloves, minced

½ C cider vinegar

¾ C packed dark-brown sugar

¼ C pure maple syrup

In a large skillet, cook Bacon over medium high, stirring occasionally, until fat is rendered and Bacon is lightly browned, about 20 minutes. With a slotted spoon, transfer Bacon to paper towel to drain.

Pour off all but 1 tablespoon fat from skillet. Add onions and garlic, and cook until onions are translucent, about 6 minutes. Add vinegar, brown sugar and maple syrup and bring to a boil. Stir with a wooden spoon, about 2 minutes.

Add Bacon and stir to combine.

Transfer mixture to a 6-quart slow cooker and cook on high, uncovered, until liquid is thick, 3 1/2 to 4 hours. Transfer to a food processor; pulse until coarsely chopped. Let cool, then refrigerate up to 4 weeks.

Bacon Pancake Donuts

1½ C flour

1 tsp baking soda

¼ tsp salt

2 Tbsp brown sugar

4 Tbsp maple syrup

½ C buttermilk

1 egg

Frosting:

½ C powdered sugar

1 Tbsp maple syrup

1 Tbsp 1% milk

Topping:

4 slices Bacon, chopped

Preheat oven to 350.

In a medium bowl, combine flour, baking soda, salt and brown sugar. Form a hole in the middle of the flour mixture then mix in maple syrup, buttermilk and egg.

Spoon two tablespoons of the donut mixture into the donut pan. Bake at 350 for 12 minutes.

While the donuts are baking cook the Bacon over the stove top until crispy. Drain on paper towels then cut into chunks. Make the frosting: in a small bowl combine the powdered sugar, maple syrup and milk.

Let the donuts cool once they are done baking in the oven. Dip the donut in the frosting mixture and sprinkle the Bacon on top.

Makes about 10 donuts.

Bacon Quiche

1 pie crust

10 slices of Bacon chopped

    (save 2 for garnish)

6 large eggs

¼ C heavy cream

¾ C milk

1½ C colby & monterey jack cheesse

¼ tsp of both salt and pepper

Cook Bacon at 425 for 20 minutes, then cut into small pieces

In a bowl mix together the eggs, cream, milk, cheese, salt, pepper and Bacon.

Lower the temperature of the oven to 350. Bake the pie crust in the oven for 20 minutes.

Take out the pie crust and pour in the egg mixture.

Bake for an additional 30 minutes. The eggs should be set in the middle when done. No wobbling. Garnish with leftover Bacon.

Fig & Bacon Pop Tarts

1 pie crust

1 jar fig jam

5 strips Bacon

1 egg

Cook Bacon and drain on paper towels, then chop.

Roll out the pie crust, then using a pizza cutter, cut into equal size squares.

Spread the fig jam on top of the pie crust; then sprinkle the Bacon on top of the jam. Do not spread jam on all of the pie squares.

Cover with another piece of pie crust cut to size over the crust with jam. If the pie crust doesn't stick, use water or the egg wash to help the crust stick together.

Using the edge of a fork, press on on the edge of the pop tart to make ridges.

Brush the top of the pop tarts with egg wash.

Bake in the oven for 20 to 25 minutes at 350 degrees.

Bondage

"Miscellaneous"

Bacon Bits

1 lb Bacon

salt & pepper

Cut Bacon into small size bites. Season with salt and pepper.

Cook Bacon until crisp.

Pulverize the Bacon in a food processor until the Bacon is about the size of peas. If you don't have a food processor, chop the Bacon up into really small pieces.

Bacon Brown Sugar Rub

1 lb Bacon, crispy

½ C brown sugar

2 Tbsp smoked paprika

1 Tbsp cumin

Cook Bacon until crispy and drain on paper towels.

In a food processor, pulse the Bacon until it's the size of salt.

Add in next 3 ingredients and pulse again until well blended.

Store in the fridge.

Bacon Butter

1 stick unsalted butter,

   room temperature

5 strips Bacon, chopped

¼ C parsley, chopped

¼ C fresh chives, chopped

2 garlic cloves, minced

In a bowl combine all ingredients.

Place the butter on saran wrap; mold the butter into a log shape.

Store in freezer or refrigerator.

Bacon Cupcake Martini

2 oz Bacon Toroni syrup

1 oz cake flavored vodka

8 oz chocolate martini mix

1 strip Bacon for garnish

In a glass shaker, combine the syrup, vodka and martini mix with some ice. Shake well.

Pour into a martini glass and garnish with a strip of Bacon.

Bacon Extract

10 oz vodka

2 oz Bacon grease

Measure out 2 oz of liquid Bacon grease and pour into a jar.

Add 10 oz of your favorite vodka.

Seal the jar and store in a dark place for a few days.

Shake once in a while.

After 3 days take the Bacon extract and place in the freezer for about 2 hours. You will see all the fat at the top of the jar. Strain the fat off and you now have Bacon extract.

Store in the fridge.

Bacon Mayonnaise

1 large egg yolk

pinch of salt

1 tsp dijon mustard

1 Tbsp lemon juice

¾ C strained & liquefied

    Bacon grease

Place egg, salt, mustard and lemon juice in food processor and pulse to mix.

Turn processor motor on and begin adding liquid (not hot) Bacon grease very slowly at first.

Once Bacon grease has been completely added, stop the food processor and taste. If needed, add more lemon juice or salt.

Cover and store in fridge for up to 5 days.

Bacon Peanut Butter

2 C peanuts

6 strips Bacon, crispy

In a food processor puree the peanuts until the peanuts have become a peanut butter consistency.

Add in Bacon and pulse until the Bacon is well blended with the peanut butter.

Store in air tight containers and in the fridge. Stir before using for even consistancy.

Bacon Pesto

1 lb Bacon, crispy

¼ C peanuts

¼ C chives, chopped

1 dash both salt & pepper

2 Tbsp olive oil

Cook Bacon until crispy; 425 for 20 minutes.

Add Bacon, peanuts, chives, salt and pepper into the food processor and pulse.

Pour the olive oil into the food processor while the Bacon and peanut mixture is pureeing, until the mixture resembles a pesto.

Serve on top of pasta or spread on bread.

Bacon Popcorn

1 bag microwave popcorn

½ stick butter

1 - 2 Tbsp Bacon salt

Microwave popcorn.

Melt butter in microwave.

Pour butter on top of popcorn and season with Bacon salt.

Bacon Ranch Dip

1 package cream cheese

1 package ranch seasoning mix

5 strips Bacon

lettuce

tomatoes

Fully cook Bacon and allow to drain on paper towels.

Combine cream cheese and ranch seasoning in a small bowl.

Spread the cream cheese and ranch mix in an 8 x 8 baking dish.

Top with lettuce, tomatoes and Bacon.

Brown Sugar Bacon

1 lb Bacon

1 C brown sugar

Preheat oven to 400 degrees.

Place Bacon on a wire rack with a pan under, large enough to fit the wire rack.

Sprinkle the brown sugar on top of the Bacon. Cook Bacon for 20 minutes until crispy.

Creamy Garlic Bacon Dip

2 C sour cream

½ lb Bacon prepared as Bacon bits

   (see page 47)

1 beef bullion cube or granules

2 green onions, minced

1 garlic clove, minced

Pulverise the bouillon cube into a powder (use a spice blender or old fashioned cloth & hammer) and add to the sour cream in a medium dish.

Mix thoroughly until it is fully blended. Add the rest of the ingredients and mix.

Let rest in refrigerator for at least 2 hours and then serve.

About the Authors

Benjamin Myhre's love of food and popular culture has culminated in a passion for Bacon and is the fire that sparked this book. While Ben loves Bacon, he also enjoys home canning, innovating his homemade pizzas and home brewing. Outside of cooking, Ben works in the technology industry, reads comic books, gets geeky about Star Wars, tries to make it to the gym to work off all the delicious food and blogs about popular culture on the internet. He lives in Fargo with his lovely wife, Ashley, his dog Charlie and three cats he lovingly calls "cat."

Jenna Johnson's love of cooking, food, photography, and Bacon has helped her create a successful food blog called recipe-diaries.com. She is married to her wonderful husband Ben and two cute furball children Colin and Jerry Lee. Ben gets to sample all the recipes and ideas Jenna has created for her blog and sometimes the children do too. She resides in Fargo and met Ben Myhre through a friend, Ashley Myhre.

Acknowledgements

Ashley Myhre to her careful planning and editing to ensure the cookbook is at its best.
Eric Ista for his awesome creative work on the cover.
Carrie Copa for her wonderful formatting skills and illustrations.

1706860R00033

Made in the USA
San Bernardino, CA
18 January 2013